How to Draw
Cartoon
Reptiles

Curt Visca and Kelley Visca

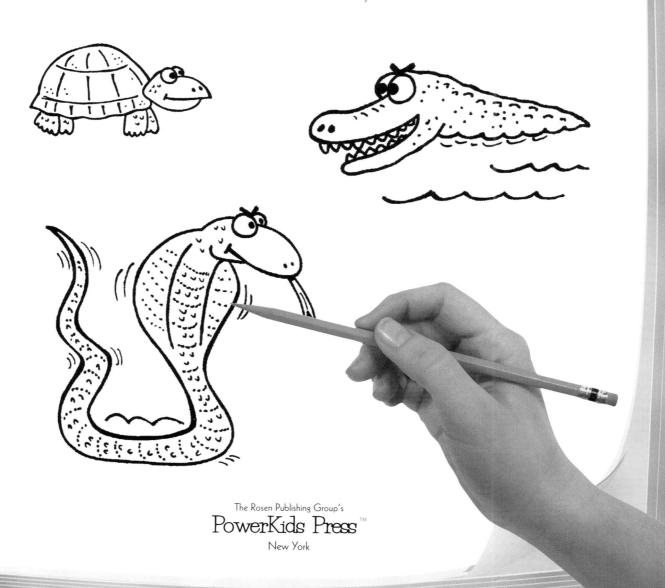

The Rosen Publishing Group's
PowerKids Press™
New York

Dedicated to Curt's dad, Norman Visca, because of all the reptile pets Curt had as a kid

Published in 2003 by The Rosen Publishing Group, Inc.
29 East 21st Street, New York, NY 10010

First Edition

Editor: Natashya Wilson
Book Design: Kim Sonsky
Layout: Emily Muschinske

Illustration Credits: All Illustrations © Curt Visca.
Photo Credits: Cover photo (chameleon), pp. 6, 8, 12 © Animals Animals/Zig Leszczynski; cover photo and title page (hand) © Arlan Dean; p.10 © Animals Animals/Marian Bacon; p. 14 © Animals Animals/Kevin & Suzette Hanley; p.16 © Animals Animals/Allen Blake Sheldon; p. 18 © Kennan Ward/CORBIS; p. 20 © Animals Animals/A. & M. Shah.

Visca, Curt.
How to draw cartoon reptiles / Curt Visca and Kelley Visca.
  p. cm. — (A kid's guide to drawing)
Includes bibliographical references and index.
Summary: Provides facts about different kinds of reptiles, as well as step-by-step instructions for drawing cartoons of each one.
  ISBN 0-8239-6160-5 (alk. paper)
1. Cartooning—Technique—Juvenile literature.
2. Reptiles—Caricatures and cartoons—Juvenile
literature. [1. Cartooning—Technique. 2. Reptiles in art.] I. Visca, Kelley. II. Title. III. Series.
  NC1764.8.R46 V58 2003
  743.6'79—dc21
                            2001004325

Manufactured in the United States of America

CONTENTS

Cartoon Reptiles

Reptiles are a large group of animals that includes snakes, lizards, turtles, and crocodiles. Reptiles are covered with scales. Most lay eggs to **reproduce**. They are **cold-blooded**, which means reptiles need to be in the sun to warm themselves. To stay alive, they cannot get either too hot or too cold. There are more than 7,000 **species** of reptiles. They live in every **habitat** except in polar areas, which are too cold.

Some of the reptiles in this book are record holders. The largest reptile is the saltwater crocodile, which can weigh 3,300 pounds (1,500 kg) and can grow to be 23 feet (7 m) long. The smallest reptile is the gecko of the British Virgin Islands, which reaches only 7/10 inch (18 mm) in length. The **reticulated** python and the anaconda share the record for the longest snake. Both snakes can grow to be 33 feet (10 m) long. The biggest turtle is the leatherback, a sea turtle that can measure from 4 to 8 feet (1–2.5 m) long.

In this book, you will learn many remarkable reptile facts. You'll also be able to follow step-by-step directions to draw cartoons of eight different reptiles. Cartoons are not meant to look exactly like their subjects, so feel free to add details to make your cartoons fun. As you work, don't worry if your drawings don't look just like the ones in the book. Everyone's drawings are different!

Please gather these supplies to draw your cartoon reptiles:

- Paper
- A sharp pencil or a felt-tipped marker
- An eraser
- Colored pencils or crayons to add color

The directions under each drawing will help you to add new parts to your cartoon. The Terms for Drawing Cartoons list on page 22 explains the drawing shapes. Take your time and practice your cartoons. Soon you will be a creative cartoonist!

Some slithering, creeping, snapping reptiles are waiting for you to draw them. Get ready!

The Rattlesnake

Rattlesnakes are poisonous reptiles. The rattles on the ends of their tails are made of hollow rings. A new ring grows every time a rattlesnake **molts**. Rattlesnakes molt up to four times a year. The rattle makes a rattling sound when rattlesnakes shake their tails to warn **predators** to stay away. Rattlesnakes make their homes in hot, dry areas of North America and South America. They eat **rodents**, birds, and lizards. At night a rattlesnake coils up and waits for its **prey**. The rattlesnake senses an approaching animal's body heat, and strikes. The snake bites the prey with two hollow teeth, called fangs. **Venom** comes out of the fangs to **paralyze** the prey. The rattlesnake then opens its jaws wide and swallows its food headfirst.

1

Begin by drawing an oval and a backward letter *C* for the eyes. Add a dot inside each eye. Make a letter *V* above the eyes.

2

Start from the eyes and draw a curved line and a straight line for the top of the mouth. Make curved vertical and straight lines to finish the mouth. Add a letter *U* for the jaw.

3

Incredible! Draw another slightly curved vertical line for the other side of the mouth. Add straight lines for shading. Draw a small letter *W* in the top of the mouth for the fangs.

4

Starting behind the eyes, make a long curved line for the top of the rattlesnake. For the bottom of the snake, make another long curved line, starting at the rattlesnake's jaw.

5

You did an excellent job! Draw three small ovals and a little, upside-down letter *U* at the end of the snake for the rattles.

6

Draw letter *V*'s filled with dots on the snake's back. Add small letter *U*'s, dots, and action lines to the snake. Make the ground using ovals and wiggly lines.

The Cobra

Cobras are snakes that are known for their hoods. When a cobra is threatened or excited, it flattens the ribs of its neck so they stick out around its head to form a hood. When a snake charmer plays music for a cobra, the cobra opens its hood and seems to dance. Actually the cobra does not hear the music. It follows the snake charmer's movements while rising up nearly one-third of its total length.

Some cobras catch their prey with **venomous** bites. Some blind their prey by spitting venom into the prey's eyes. King cobras are the largest of all venomous snakes. They live in Africa and Asia and can be 18 feet (5.5 m) long. The venom in one king cobra bite can kill 1 elephant or 20 people!

1

Let's start by making a circle for the first eye. Draw a dot inside the eye. Add a long letter C with a short straight line at the end.

2

Draw two curved lines for the head and the jaw. Add a curved line and a dot for the other eye. Draw a letter V above the eyes. Make two lines and a letter V for the tongue.

3

Outstanding work! Draw two slightly curved vertical lines to begin the cobra's body. Add two wider curved lines for the cobra's hood.

4

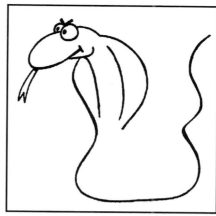

Draw a long curved line for the front of the cobra's body and tail.

5

Wow! Add another curved line for the back of the cobra. Connect the end of the line to the end of the first curved line to make a pointy tail.

6

Add small letter U's and lines of dots to your cobra. Make action lines. Draw a sandy ground. Great!

The Python

Pythons are very large snakes that live mostly in **tropical** habitats. A python can weigh more than 300 pounds (136 kg)! Pythons are great at swimming and at slithering up trees. They hide in the leaves to wait for prey. A python smells its next meal with its forked tongue. The tongue brings scents from the air to a special part in the python's mouth that senses smell. When a monkey or other kind of prey gets close enough, the python captures and **constricts** it. This means that the python wraps itself around the animal and squeezes it until it can't breathe. As pythons grow larger, they eat larger animals, such as goats and pigs weighing as much as 100 pounds (45 kg)! Once a python has eaten, it isn't hungry again for weeks.

1

Begin by making a circle and a letter C for the eyes. Add a dot inside each eye. Draw a letter V above the eyes for a fierce look.

2

Start by the eyes and make a curved line and a backward letter C for the mouth. Add a curved line for the bottom jaw. This python will be eating a rodent.

3

Draw a short line from the top of the snake's mouth. Add two curved lines for the rodent's tail. Make two curved lines for its belly. Add straight lines and zigzag lines for its feet.

4

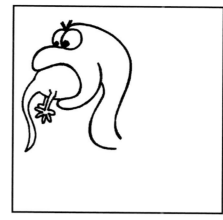

Add a curved line for the back of the snake's head and a curved line for the neck.

5

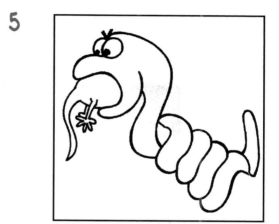

To make the python look like it's wrapped around a tree, use curved lines to make four sections of snake. Add an upside-down letter U for the tail. It was tricky, but you did it!

6

Make curved triangles and dots on your snake. Add action lines. Use curved and zigzag lines to add a tree branch, a hill, trees, and grass.

The Chameleon

Chameleons are lizards that can change colors. When a chameleon is excited, afraid, cold, or in the shade, it gets lighter in color. When a chameleon is warm, angry, or in bright light, its skin darkens. The skin can turn shades of brown, gray, and green. Chameleons are from 1 to 25 inches (3–63 cm) long. Their eyes stick out from their heads and can move in different directions. Chameleons can look forward and backward at the same time!

Chameleons live in trees and bushes. They use their curled, **prehensile** tails and toes to grasp branches. Chameleons use their long, sticky tongues to catch insects. Their tongues can be longer than their bodies!

1

Draw a circle for the chameleon's eye. Make a dot inside for the pupil and four short curved lines for detail.

2

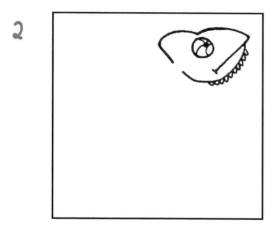

Make a curved, upside-down letter V above the eye. Add a curved line and a sideways letter T for the mouth. Make a wide letter U for the jaw. Add small letter V's underneath.

3

Great work! Draw a curved line for the back and upside-down letter V's for spines. Make curved lines for the legs and thin letter U's for the toes. Add curved lines for the stomach.

4

To make the chameleon's prehensile tail, draw two spiral lines. Continue the small letter V's from the back for more spines.

5

You're awesome! Make the second front and back legs with curved lines and letter U's. Don't forget to leave room for a tree branch.

6

Add small letter U's and lines on your chameleon. Draw tree branches. Make leaves using two straight lines and four thin letter U's.

The Gecko

Geckos got their name from the clicking noise one species makes. The noise sounds like "gehk-oh." Other species make barking or squeaking noises. Although they live outside, geckos often enter houses. They can run up walls and across ceilings! Sticky pads on the bottoms of their feet allow them to climb almost anything. If a snake or other predator catches a gecko by the tail, the tail breaks off. The gecko escapes and grows another tail within months. Geckos eat insects and live in warm areas around the world. Banded geckos are the most common geckos in the United States. They have yellow and brown stripes and are from 4 to 6 inches (10–15 cm) long.

1

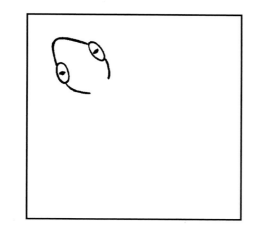

Draw a curved line for the nose. Make ovals for the eyes. Add oval-shaped dots in the eyes. Draw curved lines for the back of the head.

2

Draw two pairs of curved lines on each side of the gecko for the front legs. Make five small letter *U*'s on each leg for toes. Add a small circle on the end of each toe for claws.

3

Wonderful work! Draw a curved line on the left and a curved line on the right for the gecko's body. Start the hind legs with curved, upside-down letter *V*'s and curved lines.

4

Draw three thin letter *U*'s on each back leg for the toes. Add small circles for claws. Make another curved line to finish each back leg.

5

You are a sensational artist! To make the gecko's tail, draw two long curved lines that connect in a point.

6

To complete your cartoon, use small lines to make stripes on your gecko. Make an angled line on each side of the gecko for a tree trunk. Add dots and ovals for detail.

15

The Desert Tortoise

Desert tortoises are turtles that live only on land. They can be found in the hot, sandy deserts of the American Southwest. They can live in places where the **temperature** reaches 140°F (60°C)! In hot weather, the tortoises use their strong, flat front legs to **burrow** underground. They spend 95 percent of their lives under the ground. Desert tortoises can also survive for a year or more without water. They get water during the spring from moisture in desert plants, such as grasses and **cacti**. Female desert tortoises lay from 2 to 14 eggs at a time in nests near their burrows. Male babies hatch from eggs that **mature** at cooler temperatures. Female babies hatch from eggs that mature at higher temperatures.

1

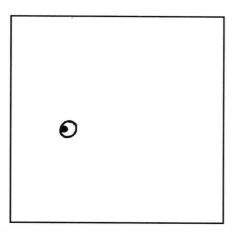

Let's begin by drawing a circle for an eye. Make a dot inside for the pupil.

2

Draw a curved line for the top of the nose. Make a sideways letter *T* for the mouth. Add a curved line for the other eye and a dot inside for the pupil.

3

Fantastic! Starting under the mouth, draw a wide letter *U* for the jaw and a curved line for the rest of the head.

4

Add a wide curved line for the top of the tortoise's shell. Make a wiggly line for the bottom of the tortoise's shell.

5

Super! Under the shell, draw two slightly curved lines with a wiggly line connecting them for the first front leg. Repeat these steps to make a back leg. Use curved and wiggly lines for the second front and back legs.

6

Add dots, lines, and small letter *U*'s on your turtle. Make cacti and grass using curved and zigzag lines. Use curvy lines for the mountains.

17

The Sea Turtle

Sea turtles appear to fly through water. They seem to move their flipperlike legs the way birds move their wings. They can reach swimming speeds of nearly 20 miles per hour (32 km/h). Sea turtles eat **crustaceans** and fish.

Usually only the female sea turtles come ashore, to lay their eggs. They will **migrate** up to thousands of miles (km) to the beaches where they were born. A female can lay more than 100 eggs at a time. As soon as the baby turtles hatch, they crawl toward the ocean. They usually move at night, when they are guided by the **reflection** of the moonlight on the water. Only 1 percent of these **hatchlings** reach the ocean. Most hatchlings are eaten by birds and other predators.

1

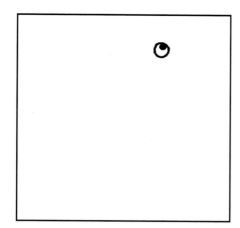

Start by drawing a circle for the first eye. Make a dot inside for the pupil.

2

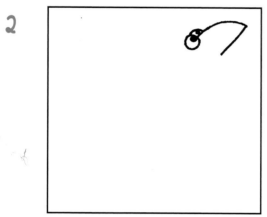

Draw a curved line and a straight line for the top of the head. Add a curved line and a dot for the second eye.

3

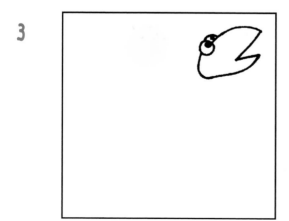

Splendid! Make another straight line to show the mouth. Add a slightly curved line for the bottom of the head. Continue the curved line with a letter C to finish the head.

4

Make a long curved line for the bottom of the sea turtle's shell. Add another curved line for the top of the shell. Draw large and small rectangles on the shell for detail.

5

You are creative! Draw two curved letter U's for the first front and back legs. Draw the other legs with curved lines. Add wiggly lines for toes and a small letter U for the tail.

6

Make dots and letter U's on the shell, the legs, and the head. Add action lines. Make circles for water bubbles and add some fish. Super!

The Crocodile

Crocodiles live in swamps, marshes, rivers, and lakes. They swim quietly through the water using their long, **muscular** tails and webbed feet. They keep their eyes, ears, and nostrils out of the water as they search for their prey. They can swallow fish, birds, and other small animals in one gulp! Crocodiles look like their **relatives** the alligators, but there are some differences. Alligators' snouts are shorter and more rounded than are crocodiles' snouts. The fourth tooth on each side of a crocodile's snout sticks out of the snout.

Crocodiles are **endangered**. They are hunted for their skin, which is made into belts, purses, and shoes. Their habitats are being destroyed, leaving crocodiles no place to live. Many laws now protect crocodiles.

1

You'll be drawing two crocodiles! Begin with a circle and a letter *C* for the eyes. Add dots for pupils and a letter *V* above the eyes.

2

Start by the eyes and make a long letter *U* for the top of the snout. Add a long, thin letter *U* for the bottom of the snout. Make wiggly lines in the mouth for the teeth.

3

Very good! Draw a bumpy, slightly curved line for the top of the crocodile.

4

Make a long wiggly line to show the crocodile coming out of the water.

5

Follow steps 1, 2, 3, and 4 to make a second, smaller crocodile. Make it swimming in the opposite direction.

6

Add lines and dots for detail on your crocodiles. Make wiggly lines for water, a long line for the shore, and curved lines for plants.

21

Terms for Drawing Cartoons

Listed below are some words and shapes you will need to know when drawing cartoon reptiles:

⟨ Action lines	O Oval
\\ Angled lines	▯▮ Rectangles
O Circle	⌁ Shade
⌒ Curved line	⊣ Sideways letter *T*
∴ Dots	◎ Spiral line
C Letter *C*	— Straight line
U Letter *U*	| Vertical line
V Letter *V*	∿ Wiggly line
W Letter *W*	Ɛ Zigzag lines

Glossary

burrow (BUR-oh) Dig holes in the ground.

cacti (KAK-ty) Spiny plants that grow in hot, dry places, like deserts.

cold-blooded (KOHLD BLUH-did) Having a body temperature that is the same as the air's temperature.

constricts (kun-STRICKS) Squeezes.

crustaceans (krus-TAY-shunz) Marine animals, such as crabs and lobsters, that have tough outer coverings, segmented bodies, and jointed legs.

endangered (en-DAYN-jerd) In danger of dying out.

habitat (HA-bih-tat) The surroundings where an animal or a plant naturally lives.

hatchlings (HACH-lingz) Newly hatched baby animals.

mature (muh-CHUR) To age or ripen.

migrate (MY-grayt) To travel a long distance from one place to another.

molts (MOLTS) Sheds skin, hair, feathers, or a shell.

muscular (MUHS-kyuh-ler) Strong.

paralyze (PA-ruh-lyz) To make unable to move.

predators (PREH-duh-terz) Animals that hunt other animals for food.

prehensile (pree-HEN-sul) Able to grasp objects by wrapping around them.

prey (PRAY) An animal hunted by another animal for food.

reflection (rih-FLEK-shun) A mirrored image.

relatives (REH-luh-tihvz) Animals that are similar to other types of animals, but that are not exactly the same type.

reproduce (ree-pruh-DOOS) To make babies.

reticulated (reh-TIH-kyoo-layt-ed) Having a skin pattern that looks like a net.

rodents (ROH-dints) Animals that gnaw things with their long, sharp front teeth. Mice, rats, and squirrels are examples of rodents.

species (SPEE-sheez) A single kind of plant or animal. All humans are one species.

temperature (TEM-pruh-cher) How hot or cold a thing is.

tropical (TRAH-pih-kuhl) Places near Earth's equator that are always warm.

venom (VEH-num) The poison in a snake bite.

venomous (VEH-nuh-mis) Uses venom as a poison.

Index

Web Sites

To learn more about reptiles, check out this Web site:
www.wc4.org/reptiles_snakes.htm